Servi

Society:

The Social Responsibility of Business

by
Simon Robinson

Senior Anglican Chaplain, and tutor in the Centre for Business and Professional Ethics, University of Leeds

GROVE BOOKS LIMITED
Bramcote   Nottingham   NG9 3DS

CONTENTS

Page
Introduction 3
1. Making a Profit 4
2. Responsibility and Service 9
3. Christianity and Business 15
4. Principles and Practice................................ 20
5. Enabling Service 23

THE COVER PICTURE

is by Greg Forster

First Impression July 1992

ISSN 0951-2667

ISBN 1 85174 214 X

INTRODUCTION

This paper is about the social responsibility of business. The topic often produces a rather incredulous reaction from the man in the street. Isn't social responsibility and business a contradiction in terms? Surely the business world owes nothing to society, and anyway it does not behave as if it did. Business is about self-interest and nothing more, so the argument goes.

Not unnaturally business people tend to resent this view, claiming it to be a stereotypic and shallow reaction to their role in society. In response they and the world of business ethics have in recent years attempted to examine more closely what business does involve, what its role in society is, how far self-interest is acceptable in this, and just what responsibility business might have, if any, to society. This is an important task not least for businesspeople, so that they can begin to frame a positive view of their contribution to society, and their work can be properly appreciated.

This paper reviews some of the arguments in this debate and pleads for a careful examination of the concept of business as service. In particular it argues for a complex view of service which sees businesspeople as having an important role to play in the very definition of that concept and of the social responsibility of business.

1. MAKING A PROFIT

In examining the the social responsibility of business it is important to begin with what might be termed the minimalist position. This argues that the role of business is the creation of wealth and that the only acceptable responsibility of business is to make a profit. The argument specifically defines social responsibility in terms of involvement in social concerns, arguing that business would be wrong to become involved in them. Such a position was put forward in an influential article by Milton Friedman.[1]

Albert Z. Carr goes further to argue that business should be run according to a particular game ethic which is set quite apart from the general ethic of society. In the light of such an ethic the idea of business as having a social responsibility has little meaning.[2]

The Obligations of the Company

Friedman's paper deals firstly with the exclusive duty that the company owes to the owners. The executive acts as 'an agent serving the interests of his principal'. The task in this relationship is first and foremost to maximise profit, and to involve the company in activities outside this would be a violation of trust, and thus be morally wrong. This argument is not concerned to argue against the right of the company to become involved in the local community, but rather that the company has the right to invest as it sees fit. There can therefore be no moral constraints upon the company to be more socially aware and no question of the rights of the community or groups within the community being more powerful than the rights of the company in the legitimate pursuit of their goals. If the company executive does wish to become involved in society Friedman argues that this is not the payment of an obligation but rather a means to achieving the company goal. Thus, 'eleemosynary' giving, such as sponsoring a community medical project is not a company fulfilling its obligations but one raising its profile in the community and improving its image with a view to improving profits. Friedman's approach is a good example of what may be termed contract ethics i.e. that any responsibilities do not exist outside of relationships, freely entered into. The individual, or in this case the company, cannot thus be coerced into fulfilling obligations which he or she has not freely accepted.

The first part of the argument comes down then to three major elements—the primacy of the goal of profit-making, something which is written into the the contract between the executive and company, the obligations of the executive within such a contract, and the freedom of the executive to pursue the company goals.

Albert Z. Carr produces a more severe argument, to the effect that the ethics of everyday encounter have no part to play in business. Carr sees the 'ethics' of business as analogous to poker, a game where participants

[1] M. Friedman, 'The Social Responsibility of Business Is to Increase Its Profits', in *Ethical Issues in Business* ed. T. Donaldson and P. H. Werhane (Prentice-Hall, 1983), pp. 239-243.
[2] Albert Z. Carr, 'Is Business Bluffing Ethical?,' in *Harvard Business Review* 46 (January/February 1968).

can quite reasonably aim to deceive other players. All such participants know the rules of the game and accept that they apply only to that situation. Carr writes,

That most businessmen are not indifferent to ethics in their private lives, everyone will agree. My point is that in their office lives they cease to be private citizens; they become game players who must be guided by a different set of standards . . . and the golden rule, for all its value as an ideal for society is simply not feasible as a guide for business. A good part of the time the businessman is trying to do unto others as he hopes others will not do unto him.'[1]

On this basis businesspeople can acceptably deceive those involved in the business world, including the customer with respect to advertising. All expect to be deceived and operate accordingly. So social responsibility takes second place to the game and the purpose of the game.

Consequences and Credentials

The argument goes on to examine the mostly negative consequences of pursuing social responsibility, and whether business has the credentials to be so involved. It would involve costs which would have to be passed on to the customer, possibly to the shareholder in reduced dividends, and to the employee in reduced wages. Not only is this unfair, in penalising so many people with a stake in business, it also constitutes a form of taxation without representation or consultation, and is therefore undemocratic. Moreover, it is both unwise, because it invests too much power in the executive, and futile, because it is likely that the costs imposed by this approach will lead to a lowering of economic efficiency.

Finally, Friedman argues that the executive is not the best person to be involved in making decisions about social involvement. He or she is neither qualified in, nor mandated to pursue social goals. Without the skills and experience of social policy practitioners it is difficult to see how the executive could understand the needs of his local area or begin to determine social priorities. Such a task would be better suited to government and to local social concern groups, who are accountable for any involvement in society. For business to enter this field would also lead to a confusion of roles and a raising of false expectations.

Assessing the Arguments

1. The argument for a separate game ethic recognizes behaviour that does occur in some businesses, but this is hardly a sufficient ground to build a whole ethic of business on. It very quickly moves to a form of ethical relativism, where the ethics of business is determined by the needs of businesspeople, and is unique to them. Ultimately, the game analogy runs the danger of assuming that there is only one aim in the game of business, and moreover this is specifically to defeat the opposition.

The analogy also falls down, in that the participants in poker enter the game willingly and freely, prepared to take the risks inherent in the game. Business decisions, however, affect far more than the 'key players' in business, and the consequence of losing can lead to the loss of livelihood

---

[1] *Ibid.* pp.145-148. Note that Carr's game analogy should not be confused with game theory in management, and management studies.

without having willingly entered the game in any direct way. It must also be noted that Carr gives no guidance as to what the rules of the game actually are. Far from being explicit and therefore open to all, as in any real game, it is clear that the game rules of business are implicit or assumed and are thus open to not just interpretation, but manipulation. Finally, Carr gives no thought to the possibility of the two ethical spheres, of work and the rest of life, clashing. Businesspeople are also part of a broader moral network which may lead to the pull of different loyalties. Carr's position does not, indeed cannot, give any guidance in such a situation.

2. Friedman's argument about the duty of the company to the owners suffers from similar narrow focus, arbitrarily restricting duty to one particular group or person. It is simply not true that the duty owed to the owner is necessarily paramount. There are other claims from what have been referred to as stakeholders i.e. individuals or groups who have some concern in the continuance of the company. They include customers, shareholders, local community, the environment, the employees and so on.[1]

There is no logical, legal or moral reason why the duty of a company should be so restricted any more than the purpose of business should be restricted to profit maximization. Recent management writings recognize both the importance of considering the claims of all stakeholders and also the fact that pursuit of other goals beside profit can have long term benefits for a company and society.[2]

Friedman's characterization of ownership is simplistic. He assumes that those who have some ownership interest in business have a clear idea of the goal of the business and that all share this unitary goal. However, amongst any group of shareholders there may be different views about the purpose of business. Others who invest in companies via insurance companies or unit trusts may not even be aware of objectives and activities of the company financed by their money.[3] Thus far from a clear picture there are several different pictures with different aims and opportunities for shareholders to be aware of and ascribe to in any business.

Behind much of this approach to the social responsibility of business is the negative view of freedom, in particular defending the freedom of executives to pursue their duty to the owners from the potentially coercive claims of society.

However, even if Friedman's characterization of the owner were right, the freedom of owners is then called into question. If the owner or owners have the freedom to determine the major purposes of business, then they cannot be constrained to make profit the prime purpose of business.[4] Once the freedom of owners to determine the goals of business is accepted then the force of any argument against social responsibility, which is based on the executive violating the trust of owners who necessarily have one goal, is lost.

[1] Norman Bowie and Ronald Duska, *Business Ethics,* (Prentice Hall, 1990), pp.40-42.
[2] See James E. Post, *Corporate Behaviour and Social Change,* (Reston, 1978).
[3] See *Capital: A Moral Instrument?* (Centre for Theology and Public Issues, University of Edinburgh, St. Andrew Press, 1992).
[4] See below, chapter three, for a further analysis of freedom.

3. The consequentialist arguments in support of this view are also questionable. It is not clear, for instance, that concern for social issues would lead to a loss of economic efficiency. It is argued that building up trust with the community would lead in the long term to an increase in profits.

The question of fairness and accountability depends upon a very narrow view of contract ethics. There is no reason why through consultation with the stakeholders there should not be clear limited accountability. The extension of a contract to involve a particular commitment to some group or groups does not mean that a company is then accountable for the improvement of all social ills in their situation. Much depends here upon good consultation and communication.

Finally, the questioning of the credentials of business to become involved in society is without substance. In any given situation business might have the clearest understanding of the needs in a local community, for instance if its own workforce is a significant part of that community. However, if a company does not have clear knowledge of the needs of the local area there is nothing to prevent it finding the necessary data, again through consultation.

Such arguments then hold little sway by themselves and debate on social responsibility has moved on, away from a narrow definition of duty, to a broader view of the role of business. Lord Hailsham is reported to have decried the clerics who characterize wealth-creation as greed, instead 'We must encourage the creation of wealth as a socially responsible activity.'[1] In this view narrowing the definition social responsibility down to involvement in society or charitable distribution is to miss a central point. Business fulfils its responsibility to society by serving society, and it serves society by producing goods and wealth which supply society's needs.

Service
It is possible to distinguish two approaches to this argument. The first accepts what underlies Friedman's position, the need for the market as the most effective and efficient method of distribution. Empirical evidence is adduced to support the good effects of business pursued in the market. The second asserts an ethic of service which accepts that business is an integral part of society and should work for the good of society. In this, writers such as Griffiths and Novak consciously replace the individualist ethic of Friedman and the late F. von Hayek with a Christian, community ethic. The Bible is seen to support both the market and the community ethic.

The first argument sees the market as the most efficient method of distribution. In this it accepts the twin hypotheses of psychological egoism, and the invisible hand. Psychological egoism is not selfishness writ large, but rather a pragmatic view which accepts that the most efficient form of incentive is that which involves self-interest. This views profit as an acceptable reward for hard work, as a necessary incentive, and as

[1] Quoted in *Capital: A Moral Instrument?*, p.9.

necessary to provide continuing resources for investment in the business. The distinction here between an acceptable pursuit of profit and the unacceptable exclusive concern for profit is important and has been held as much by Tawney and Temple as well as Griffiths and Novak.[1]

The invisible hand is a hypothesis which suggests that the market is the most effective and efficient means of distribution. The contribution of business to society through the market is both to create the wealth which enables the government to provide essential services such as education and health, and to provide for society improved standards of living by making essentials and luxuries available at more affordable prices. Hence, writers such as Joseph and Sumption argue that since the Second World War the market system has led to an increase in relative equality in Britain. Business through the market has thus led to an increase in choice.[2] Given this part that business plays in the well being of society Lord Caldecote argues that such work is 'just as meritorious as work in, for example, medicine and nursing, or social work for the disadvantaged, where direct benefits to the community can be more readily identified with the Christian duty to our neighbours.'[3] Businesspeople may thus be said to be genuine servants to society. Such an argument does not preclude concern for local community issues, though it does not demand it.

The second approach advocated by writers such as Brian Griffiths accepts much of the above position. The market is the most effective mechanism for relaying information and for making the best of the resources of society. It is also a most important method of ensuring freedom and dignity, based as it is upon individual action and not requiring any coercion from government. Griffiths also accepts the underlying Lockean view of private property and liberty as essential rights to be defended. He draws on Biblical evidence to provide a doctrinal basis, especially with regards to stewardship and work, but also to support both the view of property and the market.[4] Griffiths, however, is concerned with the values that lie behind the market. The idea of the invisible hand as an amoral, automatic mechanism ignores the realities of sin on the one hand and of the central Biblical thrust of community concern on the other. It is therefore essential to replace the possessive individualism that underlies the thought of such as Hayek and Friedman with the Christian values that he has outlined. In this he sees the market as harnessing the legitimate incentives of self-interest for the good of society. Creation of wealth and the whole business enterprise would in this view fit into a very elevated view of service which depends upon the dissemination of the kind of values noted.

The next two chapters will examine these views of business responsibility as service, including the Biblical underpinning.

[1] See S. J. Robinson, *R. H. Tawney's Theory of Equality: A Theological and Ethical Analysis* (unpublished PhD thesis, Edinburgh, 1990).
[2] Keith Joseph and Jonathan Sumption, *Equality* (John Murray, 1979).
[3] Robin Caldecote, 'A Bias Against Business' in *Wealth Creation and Christianity* (Industrial Christian Fellowship, June 1990), pp.7-10.
[4] Brian Griffiths, *The Creation of Wealth* (Hodder and Stoughton, 1984).

2. RESPONSIBILITY AND SERVICE

The view of business providing a service for society is important, precisely because it gives business a morally acceptable role in society and provides a clear purpose for it to fulfil. However, just as it is important to guard against a totally negative view of business it is equally important to be clear about what the idea of service involves. Without this it is possible to seek a blanket justification of the businessperson as servant which is equally unfounded.

The term 'service' is often seen as honourable and good in itself and it is all too easy to use the term as if the act of service per se was of great moral significance. In fact, it gains its moral power not from the act of service but from the purpose of the act. Thus, e.g., it is clearly reprehensible to serve a drug trafficker, however well you may serve him. The argument which sees the businessperson as providing a service has, as a premise, the clear purpose of fulfilling society's needs. However, behind that argument are several assumptions. Firstly, it is assumed that the needs referred to are clearly defined and accepted, and that the aim of fulfilling these needs has been achieved.

Secondly, it is assumed that the responsibilities of business are clear, in the context of this view of service.

Thirdly, it is assumed that the system of incentives required to enable business to serve society is both necessary and acceptable. However, all these assumptions are questionable.

A) The Purpose of Wealth Creation

It is argued that business serves society primarily by contributing to economic growth. This in turn leads to the fulfilment of society's needs. This is partly to do with the improvement of welfare and health facilities, due to resource maximization. It is also to do with consumer demand and a subsequent increase in choice, and thus improvement in the quality of life. The idea of economic growth as a primary good, however, has itself been questioned in several arguments, which may be briefly rehearsed:

1. The very idea of consumer sovereignty is considered by Galbraith, for instance, to be a myth. The relationship between consumer desires and attainable products is not a simple one. There is certainly no evidence to point to pre-existent needs or desires which the world of business fulfil in any straightforward way. On the contrary, it is argued that powerful advertising presents limited alternatives and actually shapes and creates the specific desires of the consumer.[1] The concept of the consumer is a morally ambiguous one in this context. On the one hand, it enshrines the principle of self-determination, the right of the customer to choose, and assumes that a rational choice will be made. On the other hand it is argued that the consumer is encouraged to choose not on the basis of rational criteria but in response to emotional needs and fears. In this sense it is not clear what meaning an increase in choice actually has.

[1] J. K. Galbraith, *The Affluent Society* (Mentor Books, 1958), especially chapters 10 and 11.

2. Defining needs in terms of economic needs only, is in itself debatable. Emotional and spiritual needs are equally as important as the need for food, shelter and material resources. This means that no indicator of happiness or of the quality of life and relationships can be confined to the creation and distribution of resources. Rather is it argued that creation of wealth and distribution of resources must be judged in the light of their contribution to broader ends such as the development of community and mutual responsibility. This approach raises questions then of how wealth is created and distributed.[1]

3. The concept of freedom of choice in the argument for economic growth is too narrow. Freedom here is actually defined as an increase in options. However it is not clear why an increase in options should of itself be an important good or that it necessarily increases freedom. Such a freedom would have to be relevant and meaningful. Freedom is a complex idea which involves not simply increased options but also the capacity to make decisions, freedom from economic oppression, and some consideration of the purpose of any freedom. Thus Michael Novak, echoing Tawney, can write of the freedom to do ones duty, over against the traditional views of freedom as negative or positive.[2]

4. Even if economic growth were accepted as the primary good the evidence for all prospering from economic growth is not clear cut. In Britain alone there is evidence of wide variations in distribution of income and of basic goods. Those at the lower end of the income range tend to be further disadvantaged by lack of opportunity and a sense of exclusion.[3]

5. The late Fred Hirsch argued that economic growth tends to lead to frustration rather than happiness or the fulfilment of desires. This is because whilst expectations are increased, positional goods such as prestigious jobs remain relatively scarce.[4] Behind Hirsch's argument are some important points about worth and status which will emerge below.

Such arguments as these make it difficult to develop a view of the businessperson as serving by simply producing goods which will be distributed in the free market.

It may of course be countered that the responsibility for distribution and the method of distribution does not lie with the business but with the market and ultimately with the government. It is the job of business to simply produce. This, however, is precisely to ignore the link between service and its end. If,as suggested above, the good of service depends

[1] A good example of such questions vigorously pursued is the 1986 Pastoral Letter by the American Bishops, 'Economic Justice for all: Catholic Social Teaching and the U.S. Economy'. The bishops were concerned for the development of economic democracy, which entailed not only full participation in economic life, but also participation in decision-making at all levels of the creation and distribution of wealth.

[2] Michael Novak, *Morality, Capitalism, and Democracy* (IEA Health and Welfare Unit, 1990) pp.16-23. See also R. H. Tawney, *Commonplace Book* (Cambridge University Press, 1970), p.56, 57.

[3] Duncan Forrester and Danus Skene (eds.), *Just Sharing* (Epworth, 1988), chapters 1 and 2.

[4] Fred Hirsch, *Social Limits to Growth* (Routledge Kegan Paul, 1977).

upon its end, then business cannot avoid some concern and ultimately some responsibility for that end. This is not to specify or prescribe how such responsibility should be carried out for any or for all businesses. It is to say that the business which seeks to serve has a responsibility to examine the end which it is serving and seek to ensure that this end is being achieved, if not directly by the business then by some other agency. All of this requires that the end of any service is articulated and the values which it represents are clarified and examined.

B) The Responsibility of Business

Business can affect society for good or for bad. The lines of causation may not always be clear, and responsibility for any effect may lie with more than business or more than one business. Equally, as noted above, there are also different views as to what constitutes a good effect. However, what cannot be denied is that because business is a part of society it forms relationships in that society, implicit or explicit, and that it has some impact on society, for which it bears responsibility. As noted above stakeholder theory points to a whole network of groups which may be affected by business: employees, customers, community, environment, shareholders, other businesses, the government and so on. In this the company is analogous to an individual who is a part of a network of moral relationships, each making some claim upon it. Faced by this array of stakeholders it is tempting to delimit the area of responsibility owed by the company, perhaps to one or two major stakeholders, as Friedman attempts to do. However, as Keith Davis notes in his 'Five Propositions for Social Responsibility' there are no grounds for ignoring the claims of the various stakeholders a priori. On the contrary not only are companies, like individuals, part of a network of moral relationships, they also owe a debt to 'society' and the various stake holders precisely because they depend upon them for purchasing their goods and enabling them to produce such goods. Also 'social responsibility arises from social power', i.e. business has been given great power within society and any such power demands sensitive, responsible use.[1]

It is equally tempting along with such as Bowie to see the responsibility of the business to produce what is deemed necessary to society, and with regards to stake holders to simply aim to avoid harm. Bowie contrasts this with the action of positively doing good.

However, reality is far more complex than that, with several different kinds of claims on business, each of which has to be addressed on its own merits and many of which go beyond the definition of responsibility as simply avoiding harm. The customer and the employee have a claim on business which involves standards of quality in behaviour and in product. In one shape or form such claims are based upon contracts, and such contracts tend to emphasize the avoidance of harm.

However, the contract does not of itself delimit social responsibility. As R. H. Tawney noted, with respect to relations at work and beyond, there is the much broader claim, that of human dignity and equality of respect.[2] The

[1] Keith Davis, 'Five Propositions for Social Responsibility' in *Business Horizons*, Vol. 18 [June 1975], pp. 19-24.
[2] R. H. Tawney, *op. cit.*

same principle applies to any stakeholders in business. Such a principle cannot be limited to the idea of avoiding harm. Indeed it is precisely about discerning and pursuing the good of the individual or group in their situation.

In the case of the environment, whilst there are laws which provide a form of contract, the emphasis is far more on the good of the environment, which actually transcends the concerns of particular groups. The environment is the basis of a functioning society and therefore the concern of all. Moreover, the more work is carried out to improve the environment the more the distinction between avoiding harm and doing positive good is blurred, precisely because it is a contribution to the good of the whole, and is ensuring and possibly improving the quality of the environment. In this context business becomes necessarily more proactive and interactive, not simply reacting to the bad effects which it may cause, and this in turn demands more consultation with stakeholders. The more that consultation occurs the more value perspectives, relevant data, and possible options are shared, and the more the language of avoiding harm or causing positive good is replaced by the language of planning for appropriate ends, ends shared by all.

Consultation is also necessary because the responsibility for any effect upon society or the environment may in fact be shared by several parties. A good example of this is the air pollution caused by motor vehicles in cities. The responsibility for this is shared by local and national government, the car industry, and city businesses in general. Providing a solution and ensuring that the solution is sustainable requires therefore a partnership of all those responsible. This principle of partnership may even extend to high levels of cooperation between businesses, such as enabling other businesses to control industrial waste.[1]

Finally, it must be noted that business may not simply affect the various stakeholders in material ways, it may also affect values held in society. Hirsch in particular argues that the market ethos within which business operates tends to erode the central community values of trust and mutual obligation. Rather does it emphasize individualism and competition, setting up status goals based upon materialism. Regardless of whether one accepts this argument or prefers the argument of Novak, i.e. that the market situation actually encourages the growth of community[2], it is clear that as a powerful member of society business both expresses values and principles, implicitly or explicitly, and that it does have an effect upon values held. This reinforces the argument outlined above that a business cannot avoid responsibility for the values and principles that, implicitly or explicitly, are involved in any service.

C) Incentives
The role of the businessperson as servant of society does not fit very easily with the the arguments about incentive and self-interest. If the professional businessperson can be compared to the caring professions in a vocation of service then it is not clear why he or she should receive so

[1] *The Economist,* 1990, September 8, p.29ff.
[2] Michael Novak, *op. cit.,* pp.12-15.

much greater financial reward, nor why there should be such wide disparity of financial rewards even within business. Given that some form of positive reinforcement is necessary for any task to be sustained, the argument for higher financial rewards for business assumes that financial rewards are necessary, with particularly high rewards for those in a position of responsibility. By implication then it also assumes that, in Clifford Longley's words 'people are not driven hard enough to honest graft and creative industrial enterprise simply by an appeal to the common good'.[1] In other words it is not realistic to expect individuals to depend upon intrinsic rewards, such as pride felt in serving a significant purpose, or non-financial rewards, such as the conferring of a higher status.

Three points may be made in response to this. Firstly, it has been assumed in the past that the caring professions have gained a high degree of intrinsic reward which is directly related to the fulfilling a sense of service. Consequently this has led them to acceptance of less high financial rewards than in business. There is no obvious reason why a business world which serves society should not also develop intrinsic and non- financial incentives, and reduce the reliance upon purely financial ones. Such work would require close attention to community at work, from the scale of the community to a developing of common purposes. Central to this would be the development of what Rawls recognizes as the prime good of self-respect, which in turn Tawney sees as depending upon what an individual gives and how he treats others quite as much as upon what he receives or how he is treated by others.[2] In this light the intrinsic rewards of service can be seen as self-interest properly understood. The common good here would not be the tired concept that Longley would suggest but rather something which could be given particular expression, and thus truly owned, by all members of the work force. In a situation where responsibility is felt to be shared it can be a powerful motivating force, harnessing what Bowlby refers to as 'the capacity for cooperation which exists in human nature'.[3]

Secondly, much of the writing on financial incentives is not clear. If they are necessary in themselves then there would seem to be no argument against high incentives and high pay differentials. If however, incentives were offered within the shared view of service there is no reason why financial rewards should be necessary in themselves, and thus no reason why there should be wide differentials.

Thirdly, wide differences in financial rewards can have a divisive effect upon community, both in the workplace and beyond. By implication they affirm financial reward as the main measure of personal value, and thus undergird a view that those who are lowest paid are of the least value. It is therefore difficult to see how wide variations in financial rewards can be seen as instrumental to a greater social good such as community. None of this is to suggest that there should be absolute equality in financial rewards, but rather acceptable relative equality within the context of shared purposes. Simply to suggest that self-interest should be used to further values such as service, which Griffiths proposes, does not address any of these issues.

[1] Clifford Longley, 'The Business of Investing in Faith', in *Wealth Creation and Christianity* (Industrial Christian Fellowship, June 1990), pp.14-17.
[2] R. H. Tawney, op. cit., pp.56, 57.
[3] Ronald Bowlby, 'Wealth Creation', in *ICF Quarterly*, Autumn 1990, p.17.

Once again then it is suggested that the old terms in which the debate is couched are no longer adequate. The general argument about whether self-interest is acceptable or not becomes overtaken by the more pressing question as to what is the most appropriate response in any particular company which seeks to serve. Once again, in looking for appropriate incentives the company has a responsibility to look beyond the simple use of financial rewards and to explore other forms of incentive tied to service. Once more this demands that the company thoroughly examine the meaning of that service and the values that sustain it.

Conclusions

The view that business can simply serve society through the market mechanism cannot be accepted as it stands. It raises questions about the effectiveness of the market and the aims of economic growth. Furthermore, a business which seeks to serve must take some responsibility for the end of that service and the principles and values behind it. Business is also responsible for its effects upon society, seen in terms of various stakeholders. Equally a business which serves is responsible for working out the relationship between service and incentives.

This argument concludes that the issue of social responsibility cannot be restricted arbitrarily. To see it purely in terms of the company being involved in social concerns or charitable giving is to ignore a prime social responsibility of producing goods for society. Such service, however, is dependent upon the purpose and means of production and demands attention to the claims of all the stake holders. Such stakeholders may also have some degree of social responsibility, and consultation is required both to determine this and to determine how best to fulfil the responsibility. This demands not simply a proactive stance but a genuine interactive stance where social responsibility is not determined beforehand but rather discovered through rigorous shared examination of principles, values, aims, the context and the options.[1] This in turn demands cooperation and enabling procedures and means that social responsibility cannot be simply seen in terms of avoiding harm. All of this has implications not simply for society but also for the company itself, not least in how it determines its own aims and objectives. In this sense the organisation of the company and the part that the employees play in determining and fulfilling the aims of service are a part of any consideration of social responsibility, not least because how a company organizes itself, and how it and its members function in a creative and responsive way will have implications for how it fulfils its responsibility to serve society.[2]

[1] See William Frederick, Keith Davis and James Post, *Business and Society* (McGraw-Hill, 1988).
[2] This view is close to that of Clarence Walton who sees the business enterprise as analogous to that of the artist. Business in this light is a social institution which provides opportunities for experimentation and problem solving, and which demands a creative response from the businessperson. C. Walton, *Corporate Social Responsibilities* (Wadsworth, 1968), p.137.

3. CHRISTIANITY AND BUSINESS

There is much Biblical support for the view of business as serving society. God gives man dominion over nature and the task of stewarding the resources of the world [Genesis 1.26-30, 2.15]. There is also a very positive view of work which sees God as the one who works, with man's work as derivative and secondary.[1] God calls man into a creative partnership, and there is an obligation to work [2 Thess. 3.6-13]. Equally, the stewardship of individual talents is to be developed and man is held accountable for this. Such stewardship of God's creation is also for the needs of the community at large. Thus from the prophets to the early fathers there is a strong emphasis upon the distribution as restitution of what is in fact a common wealth.[2]

In all this there is little evidence to support the view of business as serving society by simply operating through the market mechanism. Griffiths argues that because Jesus used the market as teaching examples at some points he did not therefore disapprove of the market.[3] However, not only is it difficult to argue from silence, it also sets a poor precedent for interpreting other parables. Did Jesus, for instance approve of the unjust judge? Even if there were approval from Jesus it is not clear that the market referred to has any resemblance to the free market of the twentieth century.

Based upon the Biblical prohibitions of theft Griffiths also argues for support of inviolable rights to private property. Such rights, he argues, are also rooted in creation. Man was created a responsible being and the freedom implied in this, including the freedom to make choices could only be 'guaranteed by the existence of private property rights'.[4] Property rights are therefore seen as 'the appropriate Christian starting point' and they in turn demand a market economy.

However, it is not clear that private property rights guarantee the freedom that Griffiths looks for, nor that the market economy is the logical outcome of such rights. It is not clear either that the Biblical evidence supports the notion of private property rights as such. In fact a radically different ideal and perspective is revealed.

1. The created world and all its resources are a gift of God and remain his. There did develop a right to family property [1 Kings 5.5, and 21], but God retains the overall property right. There is a sense then in which all property is provisional, something reinforced in the Old Testament by the ideals of the Sabbatical and Jubilee year Exodus 21.1, 23.20-21, Deut. 15.7-11, Lev. 25.8-19.]. In the New Testament this provisionality is sharpened by the eschatological perspective, so that those in business, 'whose life is buying and selling things', should 'live as though they have nothing of their own' [1 Cor. 7.30]. Schrage comments on this passage

---

[1] Alan Richardson, *The Biblical Doctrine of Work,* (SCM, 1963), pp.11-14.
[2] Duncan Forrester and Danus Skene, *op. cit.* p.73. Charles Avila, *Ownership: Early Christian Teaching,* Sheed and Ward, 1983).
[3]. Griffiths refers, for instance to the Parable of the Vineyard.
[4] B. Griffiths, *op. cit.* p 100.

that there is no question of refraining from business, just as there is no explicit condemnation of the idea of private property. However, business-persons are to refrain 'from thinking that they have future disposition over what they bought'.[1] The Gospels also give no positive support to the concept of inviolable property rights. Property was simply not thought of in those terms. Mealand identifies that radical early phase in the Gospels where Jesus proclaims God's kingdom, an end to Satan's rule, and justice for the poor.[2] This proclamation did not imply the total renunciation of possessions, any more than Acts 2.44 or 4.32-37 point to a forced communism, but rather that such resources should be used to serve the growing community. In such a context the idea that 'anyone should have an unrestricted right to private property' would never have entered Jesus' head.[3] It is precisely in such a context, alongside the framework of Jewish creation theology, that the prohibitions against theft have to be viewed. Such prohibitions represent respect for the individual within the covenant community and possibly also a concern for order within that community, rather than an affirmation of private property rights.

As the church grew and came into contact with other cultures and social structures its message appears less radical. Indeed in the Pauline communities there is a marked contrast between the early radical view of equality and justice for the poor and what Theissen refers to as 'love patriarchalism' where a relational equality is centred in the Christian community and the *status quo* is accepted.[4] Nonetheless, there is equally no simple support for the *status quo*, as John's attitude towards the 'world' shows.[5]

2. Property was also functional, with the purpose of satisfying the needs of the self and others. This is a thoroughly communitarian approach which sees God as providing for all. In the wilderness the pilgrim community moved towards their goal dependent upon God for the provision of resources in a place of scarcity [Exodus 16.18]. That provision was sufficient for the needs of all, provided that it was equitably shared. That exodus experience of dependence and sharing was central to the Hebrews' expression of the godly community causing them not only to offer the first fruits of their labour to God but to reach out to the needy in their community and beyond to the stranger in their midst [Deut. 26.7-11].

The life of the post-exilic community was radically different. Socio-economic divisions opened up, leaving individuals and small families at risk from economic pressure. Accordingly, mechanisms for reasserting the strong sense of social equality found in the pre-exilic tribal communities were set in place, such as the Sabbatical Year or the year of the Jubilee, referred to above. Whilst there is doubt as to whether these laws were put into practice they clearly reassert an ideal of distribu-

---

[1] Wolfgang Schrage, *The Ethics of the New Testament* (T. and T. Clark, 1988), p.231.
[2] David Mealand, *Poverty and Expectation in the Gospels* (SPCK, 1986), pp. 92-93.
[3] W. Schrage, *op.cit.* p.105.
[4] Gerd Theissen, *The Social Setting of Pauline Christianity* (T. and T. Clark), pp.137-140.
[5] W. Schrage, *op. cit.* p.231.

tion in and for the community which goes beyond any idea of a crude welfare state simply catering for the needy. The emphasis is rather on the common wealth as being for the good of all, and from this comes a concern for the poor. This became established in a complex of rights, such as the right of the poor to take gleanings.[1] It was further reinforced by the prophetic response to the abuses of the covenant community. They stand out against systems of economic oppression which led to a concentration of property in the hands of a few and the rights of the poor being ignored [Amos 2.6ff, Isaiah 10.1]. In such a community functionless accumulation of wealth was directly against the covenant relationship in which human beings accepted responsibility for God's creation [Is. 5.8].

Finally, the Old Testament offers the eschatological vision when all wrongs will be righted and community truly restored [Ezekiel 47.13]. What emerges from this is a view of community which is one of mutual dependence or interdependence along with a dependence upon God. Such a community also looks to mutual responsibility and a concern for the rights of all.

The New Testament view of community deepens and develops this, stressing that not only the stranger in the midst but also the neighbour beyond the boundaries should be the object of concern [Luke 10.25-37]. Such love is inseparably linked with the love owed to God and to the self [Matt. 5.43-46]. The New Covenant community is commanded to exemplify this love in its care for each other [John 13.35, 2 Cor. 8.9].

None of this takes away from the individual's responsibility to earn his living. Paul in particular aims to make it clear that he does not want to be a burden to the community [1 Thess. 2.9].

He sees maintaining himself as an expression of love for the community [1 Thess. 4.9ff]. The context of this activity is also to enable the individual to give to those in need [Eph. 4.28] and is thus far from an exhortation simply to individual responsibility.

3. The Bible stresses that a wrong relationship with material resources is potentially damaging to the individual as well as to the community. In particular over concern for material resources could cut the individual off from God. Thus Christ stresses the impossibility of serving two masters [Luke 16.13]. The term Mammon used in this passage means not just money or accumulated riches but all the individual's possessions, whatever their value.

Closely allied to this is the Wisdom perspective which sees the pursuit of riches as tempting individuals into sin, with those who put their trust in fleeting wealth as fools [Sirach 34.5-6, 5.1-2, Prov. 23.4-5.]

From the Bible and Christian tradition then there emerges a complex of principles, and insights into human nature which affect business. These may be viewed under the heads of freedom, community and the frailty of human nature.

[1] See Roland de Vaux, *Ancient Israel* (Darton, Longman and Todd), p.165.

—Work is the response to God's call to stewardship. As such it is honourable and good, an extension of God's creative work.

The principle of freedom can be seen in the context of this view, freedom to respond to God's call and to participate in his work of creation. This is the freedom to serve, and freedom is found in serving. There is no basis for an individualist view of freedom simply to pursue private aims. In all this, material resources are God's and man is responsible to God for them. Thus alongside the principle of stewardship is the call to work and to enable all people to participate in God's creative work. This takes seriously the idea of freedom as tied to moral purpose, thus providing weighty support for the arguments of chapter two.

—The context of any view of property is the covenant and redeemed community in which there is concern both for the members of the community and beyond; there is mutual responsibility; and distribution is linked directly to production i.e. the purpose and outcome of service is in no way divorced from the service. The principle of equality may be viewed in the light of the idea of fellowship or community, so that equality is neither proportional nor to do simply with calculating fairness, but with a relational equality.

Relational equality is in effect the aim in any building of community, such that the equal worth of individuals is acknowledged and they are able to participate in community for the good of the whole. Community and relational equality are primary principles and not instrumental, i.e. they cannot simply be fostered to further some other end. This demands of any company that it treat all stakeholders, within and outside the company, as genuine partners in community and that it reflects upon and plans for how that community might be developed in the situation in which it is in.

None of this suggests a simple support for the free market as it is now constituted. Rather is the moral emphasis upon creative freedom and community, and the most appropriate means of enabling these to develop. In all this it is not sufficient to stress,as Novak does, that community can only occur in a situation where it is freely accepted. It is from that basis that he goes on to argue that the market, as defender of freedom is crucial to the growth of community.[1] The Biblical view of community certainly looks to an autonomous response to the saving act of Christ. Freedom, however, is also in service and in ethical terms is discovered in response to Christ' challenge and claims in and through the social and moral relationships which surround both individuals and groups [Matt. 25].

—Over-concern for material resources can be damaging to relationships, both with God and with the community. In this the Bible takes seriously the importance of attitudes and the opportunity that accumulation gives for sin to develop. The ultimate effect of the pursuit of riches is that of dehumanization, of viewing others as the means to the primary aim of aquisition. This need not point to any simplistic, direct or necessary causal relationship between riches and sin.

[1] M. Novak op. cit. p.14.

Writers such as R. H. Tawney see a variety of factors at work here, such as the influence of implicit individualist values underlying competition, the pressure of peer and management expectations, and economic pressure, all contributing to a situation in which concern for relationships both inside and outside the company becomes secondary. In addition lack of space in policy or decision making for ethical reflection can make it difficult for the businessperson to even place social responsibility on the agenda. Thus even a businessperson with the best of motives may contribute to business relationships or structures which are either not responsive or responsible.

This awareness of human frailty provides a crucial balance to any simple view of human beings as free to enter ethical contracts. It raises the question as to the need for regulation either through government or business codes of ethics. The function of such regulation would not be to coerce but to enable individuals and companies to explore social responsibility.

Conclusion
Principles can be discovered in the Bible which do have relevance to business today. These principles support the conclusions of the previous chapter that social responsibility cannot be predetermined but depends upon consultation with social partners in any situation, and that any company has responsibilities at several levels including its effects on society and upon moral meaning in society. Also the principles support the contention that social responsibility cannot be limited to the idea of harm avoidance. However, they go beyond this in that the principles of freedom to serve and community provide content for any concept of doing positive good or discovering the appropriate action in any situation. Such principles apply both to the company itself and how it is treated by government and the company and its dealings with stakeholders. In addition recognition of human frailty demands attention to company organization, and to procedures which govern the relationships of the company to its stakeholders.

Not only does all this not give support for Griffith's view of the market it also questions his reliance upon changing the underlying values of the market with only limited attempts to modify organization and procedure. There clearly needs to be both.[1]

There remain two important questions. Firstly, just how can the principles oulined above apply to business? It is the contention of some writers that such general principles cannot and should not be so applied. Secondly, even if such principles can be applied, in what way can the service which they point to be enabled whilst at the same time ensuring that the business remains afloat?

[1] See R. H. Tawney, *The Radical Tradition* (Allen and Unwin), p.140.

4. PRINCIPLES AND PRACTICE

Peter Vardy in his book *Business Morality* questions the way in which theologians and church leaders seek to apply general principles to the world of modern business. In particular he criticizes the important report 'Economic Justice for All' produced by the American Roman Catholic bishops in 1987. In that, six fundamental principles are set out which are close to the basic principles outlined above:

1. Every economic decision and institution must be judged in the light of whether it protects or undermines the dignity of the human person.

2. Human dignity can be realized and protected only in community.

3. All people have a right to participate in the economic life of society.

4. All members of society have a special obligation to the poor and vulnerable.

5. Human conditions are the minimum conditions for life in community.

6. Society as a whole, acting through public and private institutions, has the moral responsibility to enhance human dignity and protect human rights.[1]

Vardy sees several problems which are exemplified by the Bishops' report. Firstly, he argues that the stress on society and community diminishes the responsibility of the individual, so that they feel no need to act.[2] Secondly, he argues that such principles are impossible actually to put into practice. What is demanded in work is a whole set of problem-solving skills, which may require having to make the best of some difficult choices. General principles do not really inform the decisions to made at that level. Thirdly, by implication, theologians are not qualified to lay down principles about the world of business. They live in a 'secure and problem free environment removed from business realities'.[3]

Vardy's stress on practical moral decision-making is extremely important. It is true, moreover, that it is difficult to apply Biblical principles, for instance, in a straightforward way, and the history of the concept of usury illustrates this well. The injunction against usury in Deuteronomy 23.20-21 is one of the few moral pronouncements that seems to apply directly to business. However, the distinction between the brother and the resident alien, who was not charged, and the stranger with whom usury was permitted, created more problems than it solved. The desire to emphasise universal brotherhood on the one hand and the pressures of the rise of capitalism on the other eventually led to a quite different view of usury.[1] However, none of this provides an argument against the importance of framing general principles, or against their use in some way in the decision making process of a company. Several points may be made here.

---

[1] *Economic Justice for All* (National Catholic New Service, 1987). See also *Journal of Business Ethics* 7, 1988, and *Shaping Welfare Consensus* (Centre for Concern, Washington, 1988).
[2] Peter Vardy, *Business Morality* (Marshall-Pickering, 1989), p.196ff.
[3] *Ibid.* p.194.
[4] For a full history of the concept of usury see B. Nelson, *Usury* (Harvard, 1969).

1. It is wrong to say that the proclamation of general principles precludes the working out of appropriate practical decisions. General principles are by definition without particular content, and cannot be used as prescriptions in an absolute way, i.e. as applying in the same way to all situations. The specific and particular meaning of those principles in any situation precisely requires the process of moral decision-making which takes into account all the factors which Vardy wants to stress, attention to the situation, stakeholders, options and consequences, including all the demands and constraints which are involved.

Further, it may be argued that without attention to such principles the decision-making process itself loses meaning. Without some clarification of the basic values underlying any business it is difficult to arrive at an understanding of the purpose which one is serving. The underlying point here is that all social groups express basic general principles explicitly or implicitly. Unless these are clarified and are linked to the running of the business it is hard to see what moral meaning a business might have.

2. Vardy's position not only runs the risk of attenuating moral meaning in decision making, it also sets up a false dichotomy between theoretical ethics and practical ethics which threatens to exclude the businessperson or the theologian from the total moral debate. In fact, as noted above the businessperson who seeks to serve is responsible for examining the company's principles and defined purposes. Furthermore, as the responsibility is often shared for any particular effect of business, this requires a partnership both to solve any particular problems and also to define purposes together. In such a context business has a contribution to make not only in defining its own role and moral meaning as servant but also in helping to define the moral meaning of the community of which it is a part, and which it serves. The Christian principles outlined above provide support for such a view. Once again this could mean different responses from businesses in different situations.

3. Perhaps the most striking point about the principles above is their breadth and complexity. On the one hand they give no *a priori* support to any particular business or market mechanism. On the other hand they hold in tension several doctrines which are often taken to be self contradictory, with stewardship and work seen in the context of freedom and community. There is no sense in which this combination of principles could ever be fully realized. What is important is rather that they set the criteria against which progress can be measured and regularly reviewed. In all this, the complex of principles and the stress on the company clarifying its own values and responsibilities in no way constrains the moral autonomy of the individual or company. On the contrary it actually affirms moral autonomy, precisely because it does not demand adherence to a single absolute principle, any more than it demands simple application without analyzing the situation.

None of this provides a comfortable view of business and its social responsibility. It seeks both to affirm the role of business as servant and also to challenge business to respond to stakeholders in the light of the Christian view of justice outlined above. The implications of this extend to decision-making in the business world as it now is and to the institutions which shape and define the world of business. Hence, a prophetic role for individual companies cannot be ruled out. This could range from helping other stakeholders to work through their responsibilities, to helping shape an ethical code for professions, to campaigning for a change in the legal framework of business. None of this can be ruled out *a priori*. Most importantly this means that social responsibility cannot be limited purely to decision-making within the system of business as it now stands.

A good example of the problems involved in the relating principles to decision-making is the history of the Nestle infant formula controversy. Firstly, there is no doubt that from the beginnings of the company there was a strong commitment to social responsibility and in particular the prime good of breast feeding.[1] There was also a concern that the mothers who did require infant formula were not only educated in the hygienic preparation of it but also did not rely solely upon it unless absolutely necessary—a concern for the freedom of the customer.[2] Secondly, however, at the beginning of the controversy [1973] the company were less concerned with the question of community or with the consultation of stakeholders. The result was both misunderstanding on the part of some stakeholders, miscalculations on the part of the company, and the odd sight of certain crucial stakeholders unable for various reasons to play their role as partners in social responsibility. A good example of this is the use of nurses employed by Nestle to help educate women in the use of infant formula. The intention was certainly to enable those who needed the formula to make best use of it. Nonetheless, some of the material used gave the impression that Nestle were using this educative role as an undercover means of establishing a market amongst poor mothers. Ironically here much of the problem was caused precisely by Nestle taking on too much responsibility in this situation. It was hard for many of the stakeholders from church and secular pressure groups to believe that a company could both act as objective educator and as a business. Nestle arguably took over the role of the local health services, a stakeholder who lost even more credibility with stories of free gifts from the company. Nestle finally withdrew their nurses in response to pressure groups. Sadly Nestle did not see that the best way of fulfilling their felt responsibility to educate might have been precisely to enable the local health services to fulfil their moral and social responsibility, perhaps by making grants to the local health services and by ensuring that the education was monitored by independent organizations such as WHO. It is doubtful if such grants would have cost the company more than use of their own nurses, and the effect upon the company's perceived trustworthiness, to say nothing of cutting the costs of controversy, would have been immense.

The controversy involves many aspects and is still raging in some quarters. Nonetheless, this part of it aptly demonstrates the need to relate principles to decision-making and through the principles of freedom and community the importance of consultation which may enable partners to fulfil their moral and social responsibility. Enabling this is of itself would be something of a prophetic function.

[1] J. Dobbing (ed.), *Infant Feeding: The Anatomy of a Controversy 1973-1984* (Springer-Verlag, 1988) p.103.
[2] *Ibid.* p.104.

5. ENABLING SERVICE

The final question is how far can the responsive service outlined above be enabled, without penalizing companies. Already it has been made clear that such enabling must involve more than simply a change in the values underlying the market. This is not simply because of the frailty of human nature, but also because the market itself can constrain a company's attempts to work through its social responsibility. Equally, any modification of practice or organization should not be such as takes away the autonomy of the company in determining their social responsibility.

There are four broad ways in which these aims could be achieved, through government regulation, through the development of business organization, through the development of codes, and through the development of the skills and personal qualities required to be responsive to society. What follows are but examples of these approaches.

Regulation

a) The classic role of the government has been to 'hold the ring', permitting genuine competition by guarding against the economic oppression of monopolies.[1] However, government can go beyond such a role, freeing business to be responsible. A good example of this is the setting of standards for air quality control. By setting targets for all companies to achieve this ensures that companies who wish to develop pollution control policies are not penalized

b) The constitution of companies does not always encourage or enable responsible behaviour or the exercise of good stewardship. Good examples of this are limited liability companies, and indirect shareholders. Limited liability stockholder companies allow the owners to avoid responsibility for e.g. mismanagement, and thus there is no sense of responsibility for stewardship. Indirect shareholders, i.e. shareholders who have invested via intermediate groups such as pension funds, may have no idea of what work the company is involved in, or indeed what the values and purposes of the company are.

Clearly ways should be sought of clarifying the lines of responsibility in and around any company. One possibility is for shareholders to have the status of bondholders rather than having ownership rights. They could still receive dividend returns dependent on the success of the company, but would clearly not have responsibility. Alternatively the shareholder could forego limited liability but retain ownership rights. This would provide a direct incentive to act responsibly in their ownership.[2]

The Procedure and Organization of the Company

The social responsibility of the company could perhaps be first addressed through including it in any Mission Statement. Many large companies, such as Shell, include a General Purpose Clause in their Articles of Association. Such statements of social responsibility can then act as the basis for annual reviews, which could include a social audit, i.e. a systematic study of the company's actual and projected social impact.[3]

---

[1] Even in this role it is difficult for the government to enable perfectly fair competition. There still remain great differences in power within the market.

[2] *Capital* p.43. See also Justin Welby, *Can Companies Sin?* (Grove, 1992), p.15.

[3]. Social Audits are a useful way of reflecting on social impact. As Bowie notes there are difficulties in assessing such impact (N. Bowie, *Business Ethics* (Prentice-Hall, 1982), 106-112. However, a social audit could simply use mission statements and particular annual objectives to provide the criteria for assessment.

None of this need take away from the freedom of the company or of the executive. On the contrary if members of the company were involved in the development of the Mission Statement there would actually be an increase of participation and of freedom. In turn there would be a sharing of responsibility through the company leading to a increased motivation and responsiveness. Such a basis as this would provide the framework for decision-making of any executive, and again far from taking away from executive freedom would enable the executive to fulfil their duty to all parties so much better.

In addition the organization of the company would be affected in any effort to make it more responsive. The board could include representatives of the various stakeholders.[1] The organization of large companies, especially those divided into cost centres i.e. where different parts of the company have their own budget and specific economic targets to fulfil, would have to be carefully monitored, ensuring that such targets were not the only ones and did not constrain decision-making.

All such actions would keep the decision-making of the company open to public scrutiny and would enable stakeholders in and outside business to participate in shaping the moral meaning of that business.

Codes and Company Regulation

There are several arguments for professional codes or ethical codes specific to a company. Firstly, they ensure that government regulation, useful in certain contexts, does not dominate the company. Secondly, they provide a minimum of public expectation which places pressure on members of the company to be responsive. In this, codes take seriously, along with regulation and organization, the frailty of humanity, providing protection against short term pragmatic decision-making. Thirdly, they provide the basis for work with stakeholders in the determination of social responsibility, and from this the basis of developing trust between them. Once again codes based upon consultation will be more acceptable as well as providing the basis for discovering shared responsibility.

Codes have been criticized on several grounds. It is said that codes take away from the individual's responsibility.[2] Simply following codes does not encourage imagination and responsiveness, and may even be a way of avoiding responsibility. It is a short step from this for codes to become coercive. Moreover, codes tend to be neither clear nor enforceable.

However, none of these points are conclusive. No codes can apply to all situations and each therefore requires interpretation, and such interpretation will depend heavily upon any mission statement of the company. There is no logical reason why negative enforcement and positive reinforcement of

---

[1] A number of different approaches have been tried to the constituency of boards. The danger with many of them, such as the inclusion of an angel's advocate, i.e. an expert in moral decision-making, is that they take away the responsibility to think responsively from other board members. Thus, the make up of a board should be such as responsibility is shared.

[2] A good example of this is in the *Herald of Free Enterprise* disaster. The Sheen report notes a failure of responsibility at several levels, despite a clear code of practice. In this case individuals seemed to feel that they should not go beyond their role in that code, and thus did not recognize a more general responsibility. See Report of the (Sheen) court, No. 8074, Dept. of Transport, 1987.